United States
Department of
Agriculture

Forest Service

**Southern Research
Station**

General Technical
Report SRS–103

Managing Smoke at the Wildland-Urban Interface

Dale Wade and Hugh Mobley

Authors

Dale Wade, Research Forester (now retired), U.S. Department of Agriculture Forest Service, Southern Research Station, Athens, GA 30602 (www.rxfire@ ix.netcom.com); and **Hugh Mobley**, Forester (now retired), U.S. Department of Agriculture Forest Service, Southern Region and Alabama Forestry Commission, Montgomery, AL 30309.

Cover photos: Top by Steven R Miller, Saint John's Water Management District, Palatka, FL. Bottom left by Larry Kohrman, University of Florida. Bottom right courtesy of Dale Wade.

June 2007

Southern Research Station
200 W.T. Weaver Blvd.
Asheville, NC 28804

Managing Smoke at the Wildland-Urban Interface

Dale Wade and Hugh Mobley

Abstract

When prescribed burning is conducted at the wildland-urban interface (WUI), the smoke that is produced can sometimes inconvenience people, but it can also cause more serious health and safety problems. The public is unlikely to continue to tolerate the use of prescribed fire, regardless of the benefits, if burn managers cannot keep smoke out of smoke-sensitive areas. In the South, forest management organizations commonly require that plans for prescribed burns pass a smoke screening review and some States require such a review before they will authorize a burn. Current screening systems, however, do not incorporate criteria for use at the WUI. This guide describes modifications to the Southern Smoke Screening System for burns at the WUI. These modifications couple new research findings with the collective experience of burners who have extensively used the 1976 Southern Smoke Screening System. This new smoke screening system is designed for use on burns less than 50 acres in size and has undergone several years of successful field testing in Florida.

Keywords: Fire management, prescribed fire, smoke management, smoke screening, wildland urban interface.

Contents

List of Figures

List of Tables

Introduction

Periodic prescribed fire is an integral part of the management of fire-adapted ecosystems, where it is a requisite to ecosystem health. At the wildland-urban interface (WUI), it is also used to reduce hazardous fuel accumulations and to produce recreational benefits. Fire managers would like to conduct these burns without alarming nearby residents and without having smoke intrude into smoke-sensitive areas (SSAs), but smoke will likely affect people whenever fire occurs at the WUI. Smoke effects include increased anxiety because a fire is burning nearby, minor nuisances such as ash in swimming pools, temporary inconveniences such as disrupted or detoured traffic flow, and potentially serious public health and safety issues such as aggravation of respiratory aliments and reduction of roadway visibility. Smoke consists of a great many combustion products, some of which are designated as pollutants and, as such, are regulated by various Federal and State statutes (see appendix A). Readers desiring an indepth discussion of air quality regulations and the pollution caused by fire are referred to Hardy and others (2001) and Sandberg and others (2002).

The three general strategies used to manage smoke from prescribed burns, including those at the WUI are: (1) avoid SSAs, (2) disperse and dilute smoke before it reaches SSAs, and (3) reduce production of undesirable combustion products. Managing smoke at the WUI is one of the most difficult tasks a burn manager faces. This is because SSAs are within or adjacent to the burn rather than some distance away. Smoke intrusions into SSAs cause the vast majority of public complaints related to prescribed burning at the WUI. If prescribed fire is to continue to be a viable resource management option, we must make sure the public understands that fire is necessary to perpetuate fire-adapted ecosystems and that attempting to exclude this natural force has untenable long-term consequences. If the public recognizes the dramatically different long-term outcomes between these two fire management strategies, and burn managers demonstrate they can skillfully and safely apply fire, the public is likely to allow the continued use of prescribed fire.

The purpose of this publication is to build upon the knowledge of experienced prescribed burners by describing tools that have proven helpful in reducing smoke problems . For the purposes of this publication we define "experienced" prescribed burners as those who have completed the Florida Interagency Basic Prescribed Fire Course or its equivalent. Users of this guide are encouraged to review the slide presentation for the smoke management unit of that course by going to the Florida Division of Forestry Web site http://www.fl-dof.com/ wildfire/rx_training.html and clicking on "Chapter 6: Smoke Management." Alabama also has an excellent smoke management Web site; to access it, go to www.pfmt.org/fire and click on "Fire Management."

Smoke management basics are briefly reviewed below and tools to help manage smoke at the WUI are discussed. A major modification of the Southern Smoke Screening System is introduced, which can help minimize the likelihood of smoke problems when burning in the WUI. This smoke screening system for use at the WUI has been successfully used for the past 3 years by graduates of an advanced Florida fire management training course. Concepts to keep in mind and important rules for reducing smoke impacts are reviewed in appendix B. A list of suggested reading for those interested in a more detailed treatment of various smoke related topics is provided in appendix C.

Smoke Management Basics

The key to the effective use of prescription fire is to combine appropriate firing techniques and ignition patterns with favorable weather and fuel moisture conditions to produce the desired fire intensity and severity, which will, in turn, achieve the burn objectives. The prescription should, however, also consider offsite effects caused by the byproducts of combustion. Smoke management concerns usually override all other aspects of prescribed fire planning when burning at the WUI because of the proximity of SSAs. The amount of smoke that will be generated by flaming and residual combustion, coupled with the distance to SSAs, will dictate acceptable burning conditions and ignition plans. Manipulation of fuel moisture, wind direction, firing technique, and ignition pattern can usually, but not always, result in an acceptable prescription.

Smoke Production and Significance

The primary components of wildland fire combustion are water vapor and carbon dioxide, especially during the flaming phase when combustion is most efficient. Combustion is much less efficient during the smoldering and residual phases and this inefficiency results in increased particulate emissions (at least double those produced during flaming combustion). Particulate emissions are usually the pollutant of concern in wildland fires because of their impact on visibility and human health. Because most particulates are very small, they:

- Absorb and scatter light which washes out contrast and decreases visibility
- Act as nuclei to facilitate the formation of fog
- Remain suspended in the atmosphere for relatively long periods
- Enter deep into human airways where they exacerbate respiratory problems

The amount of smoke produced is directly related to the amount of fuel consumed; when fuel consumption is doubled, the amount of smoke produced will roughly double, assuming other factors remain constant. Fuel moisture is the most important determinant of the proportion of the total fuel load that will be available during a particular combustion phase. As fuel moisture increases, more heat energy has to be used to convert the moisture to steam; this slows the combustion process and increases smoke production because more of the fuel will be consumed during the residual and smoldering phases. The combustion of damp fuels generates smoke that contains a large amount of water vapor, which, although not a pollutant, has a substantial adverse affect on visibility. Remember that live green fuels and damp fuels, whether live or dead, will significantly increase the amount of moisture in smoke. Burning when fine fuel moisture is fairly low is recommended because less energy is needed to drive off moisture, which means:

- More heat energy is available to preheat additional fuels
- Fuels reach ignition temperature quicker
- More fuel is available
- Combustion efficiency is increased
- Rate of spread and flame length increase resulting in higher fire line intensity
- More of the emissions will be entrained into the smoke plume
- The plume will be lofted higher into the atmosphere

The shape, size, arrangement, stage of decomposition, and chemistry of fuel particles all influence the proportion of the total fuel bed that will be available, as well as combustion efficiency, which in turn influences smoke production. A discussion of fuels can be found on the Florida Division of Forestry prescribed fire training and education Web site at http://www.fl-dof.com/wildfire/rx training.html. Click on "Chapter 8: Fire Behavior."

Firing Technique

Backing fires have the highest combustion efficiency because the flaming front progresses through the fuel bed relatively slowly, allowing more complete oxidation of the fuel and, thus, fewer intermediate products such as volatile organic hydrocarbons, oxides of nitrogen, and other gaseous emissions of concern. Backing fires generally consume about the same proportion of the forest floor as do heading fires, but in backing fires most of the available fuel is consumed in the flaming front so smoldering after the front has passed is substantially reduced. This significantly decreases the amount of particulate matter generated.

Even though headfires are characterized by incomplete combustion, they still produce only about half as much particulate matter as does smoldering combustion. A typical headfire in southern rough consumes about 60 percent of the available fuel in the flaming phase and 40 percent in the smoldering and residual phases (Southern Forest Fire Laboratory Staff 1976). The bottom line is that headfires produce about three times as much particulate matter as backing fires. Backing fires have two major drawbacks from a smoke management standpoint. Firstly they take more time than other firing techniques to cover a given area, which means smoke will be produced over a longer time period. Secondly, when the distance between upwind and downwind control lines exceeds about 300 feet, less of the area will be burned during the middle of the day when atmospheric dispersion is normally best. For these reasons, the increased intensity of spot fires or a flanking fire is often accepted whenever prudent even though more smoke will be produced, because the smoke will be generated over a shorter time span and be lofted higher into the atmosphere. The only caveat here is that increased fire line intensity may involve more of the understory, which will result in additional emissions. As the age of rough increases, the proportion of the available dead fuel consumed in the flaming front typically decreases; this has important implications when burning at the WUI where fuel loads are usually very high.

Smoke Transport and Dispersion

Explanation of two terms will facilitate discussion of atmospheric stability and its influence over smoke transport and dispersion. Mixing height (MH) is the height to which vigorous mixing due to convection occurs and is a good indicator of the approximate maximum height to which smoke from a low-intensity fire can rise. More intense fires, however, can loft smoke above the mixed layer because it is the temperature of a smoke parcel relative to the environmental temperature that actually determines how high the smoke will rise. As a general rule, do not burn at the WUI unless the MH is at least 1,700 feet. MH becomes less important when very small acreages of short grasses (small quantity of available fuel) are involved, but if the 1,700-foot minimum is violated and a smoke problem occurs, the burner will be held responsible. On the other hand, very intense fires that quickly consume a large amount of fuel can generate enough smoke to exceed the capacity of the air to disperse the smoke efficiently, resulting in reduced visibility at ground level. When burning heavy fuel loads, such as those created when harvesting old-growth stands where much of the material is unmerchantable and thus left on site or by natural events such as high winds or severe pest infestations, increasing the MH will help mitigate potential smoke problems. MH is part of the daily fire weather forecast in many Southern States.

Transport wind velocity (TWV) is another atmospheric parameter given in the daily forecast issued by many State forestry agencies. TWV is the average horizontal wind speed and direction from the surface up to the MH and should be at least 9 miles per hour (mph) when burning is conducted at the WUI. Wind speed is usually greatest in the afternoon and increases with height. This means that as long as surface winds are at least 9 mph, transport winds should be adequate. Keep in mind that it is possible for the wind direction to vary within the mixed layer, so the direction that smoke will be carried depends upon the height that is reached by the plume.

Atmospheric stability indicates how rapidly vertical mixing is taking place in the atmosphere. The more unstable the atmosphere, the quicker and higher the smoke can rise. When burning takes place under marginally unstable conditions, the smoke plume may drop back to ground level miles downwind even though the plume was initially lifted well into the atmosphere by the heat of the fire. Atmospheric instability normally peaks during the afternoon due to solar heating of the Earth's surface and ebbs at night as the surface cools. One can bypass the task of estimating stability on a given day by using the Dispersion Index (DI) developed by Lee Lavdas (Lavdas 1986) which is part of the daily fire weather forecast in many Southern States. This numerical index provides an estimate of the atmosphere's ability to disperse smoke and is conceptually similar to the Ventilation Index but should be a better predictor of smoke dispersion (Lavdas 1986). A doubling of the DI implies a doubling of the atmosphere's capacity to disperse smoke. The DI can be computed for any time period. Daytime and nighttime DI numbers are interpreted differently because different stability classes are used in calculating the estimate. For example, a daytime DI of 40 is the commonly accepted threshold for conducting daytime burns. Nighttime values are, on the other hand, typically very low so a nighttime DI of 12 suggests unusually good dispersion, whereas a daytime value of 12 would be interpreted as poor. Fire managers also want to know the likelihood of reduced nighttime visibility when smoke mixes with higher nighttime relative humidities. Use of the Low Visibility Occurrence Risk Index

(LVORI) (Lavdas 1996) in conjunction with the DI provides them with such a predictor. Both of these tools are described below.

A more indepth discussion of meteorological variables that affect emissions can be found by going to the Florida Division of Forestry Web site at http://www.fl-dof.com/wildfire/rx_training. html and clicking on "Chapter 7: Fire Weather." Both Florida and Georgia have full-time fire meteorologists on their forest protection staffs; these meteorologists can answer weather-related questions and, upon request, provide a timely spot weather forecast for your intended burn unit.

Residual Smoke

Smoke produced after the flame front passes is a major concern when burns are conducted at the WUI. Where dead fuel loads are heavy, particularly when a heavy duff layer and/or numerous partially decayed logs are present, smoldering can continue for days, resulting in overstory tree mortality (from root damage) as well as significant smoke problems. This residual smoke remains near the ground where it is moved by eye-level wind flow (not to be confused with 20-foot surface winds). As the ground cools at night, much of this smoke will move down-drainage where it can reduce visibility to near zero at bridges.

Extensive study of archived wind data and field studies conducted by Southern Forest Fire Laboratory staff showed that in Southern States, winds are likely to blow from every direction at some point in time on any given night. For this reason, WUI burn prescriptions usually include more stringent mopup standards, often specifying mopup at least several hundred feet in from all edges.

A guideline used by some fire managers who routinely burn adjacent to homes in Florida is to allow a 12-person crew 12 hours to burn and completely mop up a 5-acre unit in a 5-plus year palmetto/gallberry rough once the prep work has been completed. They have found that for units up to at least 25 acres in size, the total amount of time they spend burning and mopping up will be about the same whether they burn the whole unit in 1 day and come back several days in a row to handle smoke complaints, or whether they break the block into roughly 5-acre blocks and burn and completely mop up one each day with no complaints. Water-and-foam is often the method of choice for mopup at the WUI, and use of smaller burn units facilitates reaching all parts of the burn.

Florida statutes allow authorized fires to actively spread between 0900 and 1 hour before sunset (1 hour after sunset for certified burners), and under certain weather conditions, a burn authorization can be obtained for a nighttime burn. We recommend that all burns at the WUI be started as soon after 0900 as conditions warrant so they can be completed early enough to allow sufficient time for mopup before sunset. Nighttime burns at the WUI should only be considered immediately after passage of a cold front, when the lower ambient temperatures will help minimize overstory crown scorch, and only

when the predicted wind velocity will not result in other fire or smoke management concerns.

Tools

Many models and tools have been developed to aid in managing smoke and additional ones are under development. A discussion of available and emerging tools can be found in Sandberg and others (2002) and at http://www.fire.org/. Tools introduced or reviewed in this publication include:

- The DI for assessing the atmosphere's capacity to disperse a smoke plume
- The LVORI for assessing the likelihood of a vehicle accident caused by poor visibility resulting from residual smoke
- A smoke screening system for managing smoke at the WUI

Lavdas Dispersion Index (DI)

The relation of the DI to burning conditions is shown in table 1. The DI is part of the

Table 1—Lavdas Dispersion Index,[a] revised on the basis of extensive use by field practitioners

Lavdas Dispersion Index	Smoke dispersion	Interpretation of daytime values
70 +	Very good	Burning conditions are so good that fires generally present control problems. Reassess decision to burn unless escape, particularly as a result of spotting, is not a problem, e.g., burn unit is surrounded by plowed fields. DI is generally too high for a WUI burn.
50–69	Good	Preferred range for prescription burns, but fire control becomes more difficult as values get higher.
41–49	Generally good	Especially when the planned burn is smaller than 50 acres. Afternoon values in most inland forested areas typically reach this range.
Reassess decision to burn at WUI if daytime DI < 41		
21–40	Fair	Stagnation may be indicated if DI is in this range and windspeed is low. Reassess decision to burn, especially if heavy rough or large dead fuels are present, or unit is larger than 15 acres.
Below 20	Poor to very poor	Do not burn at the WUI.

DI = Dispersion Index; WUI = wildland-urban interface.
[a] Lavdas (1986).

5

daily fire weather forecast produced by many Southern States.

Low Visibility Occurrence Risk Index (LVORI)

The LVORI (Lavdas 1996) shown in table 2 was developed to rank the relative likelihood of a fog and/or smoke-related accident on the southern Coastal Plain. LVORI is a function of relative humidity and the DI (table 3) based on the proportion of accidents involving fog and/or smoke, as reported by the Florida Highway Patrol from 1979–81. The LVORI is a scale from 1 to 10 with 1 indicating a low likelihood of poor visibility and 10 indicating an extremely high likelihood of poor visibility. The LVORI is a valuable tool for assessing the probability of low visibility in down-drainage areas at night or under stable atmospheric conditions. Caution should be used when contemplating WUI burns with a LVORI of 5 or higher, and WUI burns should not be conducted when the LVORI is predicted to be 7 or higher unless the fire will be completely mopped up (out—no smokes) by dusk.

Southern Smoke Screening Systems

Smoke management at the WUI is one of the most difficult parts of the burn prescription to prepare because SSAs often occur within a short distance on all sides of the intended burn unit. There will not be enough information available in the foreseeable future, nor can a burning prescription integrate all the variables necessary, to predict how much the visibility will be reduced at a given distance from a burn, or the effects it could have on human health and welfare. In fact, many of the interactions between these variables are not yet well understood. Nevertheless, most Southern States have voluntary or mandatory smoke management guidelines that should or must be followed when planning a prescribed fire. Many Southern State forestry agencies have Web sites that provide recommended and/or required procedures. State forestry Web sites can be accessed through the National Association of State Foresters Web site at www.stateforesters.org/.

Table 2—Description of Low Visibility Occurence Risk Index (LVORI) values

LVORI values	Description
1	Lowest proportion of accidents with smoke and/or fog reported (130 of 127,604 accidents, or just over 0.0010 of all accidents)
2	Physical or statistical reasons for not including in LVORI class 1, but proportion of accidents not significantly higher
3	Higher proportion of accidents than LVORI class 1, by about 30 to 50 percent, marginal significance (between 1 and 5 percent)
4	Proportion of accidents significantly higher than LVORI class 1 (by a factor of about 2)
5	Proportion of accidents significantly higher than LVORI class 1 (by a factor of 3 to 10)
6	Proportion of accidents significantly higher than LVORI class 1 (by a factor of 10 to 20)
7	Proportion of accidents significantly higher than LVORI class 1 (by a factor of 20 to 40)
8	Proportion of accidents significantly higher than LVORI class 1 (by a factor of 40 to 75)
9	Proportion of accidents significantly higher than LVORI class 1 (by a factor of 75 to 125)
10	Proportion of accidents significantly higher than LVORI class 1 (by a factor of about 150)

Table 3—Low Visibility Occurrence Risk Index (stable conditions such as at night)

Relative humidity	Dispersion Index											
	> 40	40–31	30–26	25–17	16–13	12–11	10–9	8–7	6–5	4–3	2	1
< 55	1	1	2	2	2	2	2	2	2	2	2	2
55–59	1	1	2	2	2	2	2	3	3	3	3	3
60–64	1	1	2	2	2	2	3	3	3	3	3	3
65–69	1	3	3	3	3	3	3	3	3	3	3	4
70–74	3	3	3	3	3	3	3	3	3	3	3	4
75–79	3	3	3	3	4	4	4	4	4	4	4	4
80–82	3	3	3	3	4	4	4	4	4	5	5	6
83–85	4	4	4	4	4	4	4	4	5	5	5	6
86–88	4	4	4	4	4	5	5	5	5	6	6	6
89–91	4	4	4	4	5	5	5	5	6	6	7	7
92–94	4	4	4	5	5	5	6	6	6	6	7	8
95–97	4	4	4	5	5	6	6	6	7	8	8	9
> 97	4	4	4	5	5	7	8	8	9	9	10	10

Few WUI prescribed fire projects can pass any smoke screening system now in use, but prescribed burning is necessary to perpetuate fire-dependent plant communities in the WUI. For this reason, the Southern Smoke Screening System (Southern Forest Fire Laboratory Staff 1976) has been modified to facilitate successful smoke management when burning is conducted at the WUI. The new system, the WUI Smoke Screening System, is described herein. It is based largely on extensive fieldwork conducted by Hugh Mobley, which he used to modify the original version of the Southern Forestry Smoke Management Guide. (To see the guide as modified by Mobley, go to www.pfmt.org/fire, click on "Fire Management," then click on "Smoke Management.") Dale Wade further modified the Southern Forestry Smoke Management Guide; the resulting WUI Smoke Screening System is intended specifically for WUI burns smaller than 50 acres.

For larger units, the original screening system found in The Southern Forestry Smoke Management Guidebook (Southern Forest Fire Laboratory Staff 1976) should be used. It can be found on the Web at http://www.srs. us.usda. gov/pubs/viewpub.jsp?index=683. If the intended burn does not pass that system, consider breaking it into smaller units and using the WUI Smoke Screening System.

The latter system is straightforward and is designed for use in the initial planning phase as part of the written burn prescription. It should also be used just before the burn to suggest alternatives when weather conditions are not as described in the plan. This system should not be used without a working knowledge of fire behavior and smoke management. The better one's understanding of the factors that affect smoke, the more fully and safely one will be able to interpret the results provided by this WUI screening system. Both smoke screening systems utilize many, but not all, of the major variables that affect smoke. Values are based on "worst average" weather and fuel conditions and worst case events. In some cases, indices are based on very limited research and field verification. The total amount and rate at which smoke will be produced are crucial elements in developing a burn prescription, but are at best only indirectly addressed in current smoke screening systems (including this one). For example, the effects of fuel loading by size class, fuel moisture, and fuel compaction on smoke production have only been studied on a very coarse scale. Therefore, current smoke screening systems can only suggest whether a smoke problem is likely, marginally likely, or not likely. They are a starting place to get a feel for managing smoke.

The burn manager must make the final decision. Experience and knowledge must be coupled with familiarity with the locale so the burn manager can judge whether the burn in question is likely to cause a smoke intrusion given the weather conditions and firing techniques spelled out in the burn prescription. The more experienced and knowledgeable that person is about prescription fire and smoke management, the better the decision will be.

Smoke and Nighttime Burns

As a general rule, nighttime burns should not be conducted in the WUI. The nighttime atmosphere is usually stable, surface winds are near calm and the direction of light breezes is generally variable and difficult to predict, fine fuel moisture content is higher, and inversions are common. More combustion products, particularly water vapor, are thus produced and plume rise is limited, so the smoke tends to remain much closer to the ground where it reduces visibility, especially when combined with fog. Nonetheless, nighttime burns are sometimes advocated, e.g., in young pine stands because ambient temperature tends to be lower at night. If such a situation arises at the WUI, a nighttime burn should only be considered when the weather forecast predicts steady winds lasting all night. Such conditions are usually associated with passage of a cold front. The fire and smoke should be monitored continuously and a tractor-plow unit should be onsite so that the burn can be terminated if necessary. Have lighted "smoke" signs available and make sure local law enforcement personnel are alerted. A

nighttime DI forecast can be obtained in Florida, Georgia, and several other Southern States. Interpretation of nighttime DI is entirely different from interpretation of daytime DI. At night a value of 8 or higher is generally acceptable (in selected rural areas of Florida, a nighttime DI value of 3 is permissible). Note that the WUI Smoke Screening System detailed below is *not* applicable for nighttime burns.

Gaining Experience in Smoke Management

To increase your understanding of how much smoke is produced and what happens to it in various plant communities under different weather and topographic conditions we suggest the following:

- Observe—Observe and document the production, transport, and dispersion of smoke on prescribed burns, even when no SSAs are identified. Check downwind and down-drainage to observe the smoke during the day, at dusk, before midnight, and at dawn the next morning. Document the distance to which the smoke is a visibility problem. Include all the above information in your written burn evaluation. This information can be used later when burns are conducted in the same fuel type under the same general conditions and you have SSAs to consider.

- At dusk—Always check your burn for smoke at dusk. If there is residual smoke, monitor all night unless there is very little, in which case, check again just before daylight the next morning.

- Fog-prone areas—Learn where and at what time fog generally occurs in your area. Locate and mark fog-prone areas on your administrative map.

When developing a burn prescription, check to see if the smoke plume might reach a fog-prone area. If the plume will likely reach such an area, make sure photos are taken to document the burn and smoke dispersion. If fog forms in the potential impact area the evening after a burn, monitor all roads in the area throughout the night. Be aware that conditions can deteriorate from relatively good visibility to zero visibility within a matter of minutes. Consider developing a smoke patrol plan with thresholds for specified levels of activation; Bill Twomey developed such a plan for the Francis Marion National Forest in South Carolina in the 1990s and has found it very useful.

The WUI Smoke Screening System includes estimates of minimum distances that burns should be from SSAs to minimize the impacts of smoke on these SSAs. Because data are limited, the WUI Smoke Screening System tends to be conservative. For example, prescribed burns may be smaller in size, or for some other reason produce less smoke than the system suggests. If you take the time to record and catalog the smoke results of your WUI burns, this accumulating data will allow better estimation of potential impacts of smoke on SSAs in your area.

If following any of the guidelines in the WUI Smoke Screening System results in smoke intrusion into an SSA, mitigate the intrusion and then *please* do all the following:

- Estimate the downwind extent of the problem

- Try to determine the exact cause of the problem

- Think about how you can adjust the screening system so it will not happen again

- Notify others of the problem you encountered, e.g., your local fire council, and get word back to Scott Goodrick with the Southern Research Station, Disturbance Work Unit, Smoke Management Team located in Athens, GA (http://www.srs.fs.fed. us/smoke)

The Wildland-Urban Interface Smoke Screening System

This system has five steps. Figure 1 diagrams the process.

- Step 1—Plot distance and direction of probable smoke plume and residual smoke

- Step 2—Identify SSAs

- Step 3—Deal with SSAs within the first one-fourth of the downwind and down-drainage impact distance

- Step 4—Deal with SSAs within the last three-fourths of the downwind and down-drainage impact distance

- Step 5—Interpret screening system results

Step 1—Plot Distance and Direction of Probable Smoke Plume

Step 1A

Use a map on which the locations of all SSAs can be identified and plot the footprint of the planned burn. Then draw another line around the burn 500 feet out from the edge of the burn area. This 500-foot buffer zone indicates the minimum area that is likely to be impacted regardless of wind direction. If the intended burn unit is larger than 50 acres, divide it into subunits that are less than 50 acres in size. Go to step 1B.

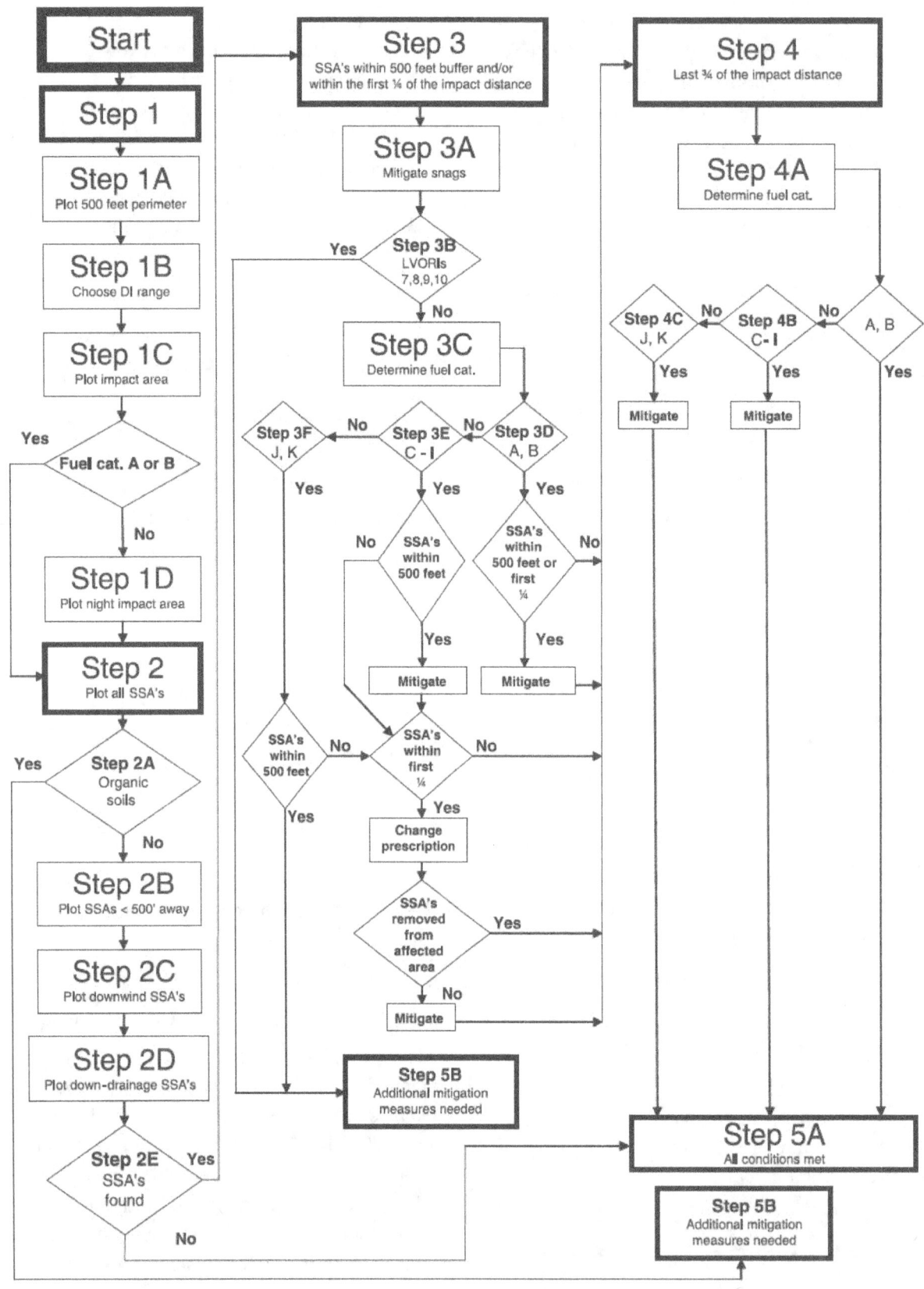

Figure 1—Flowchart of the Wildland-Urban Interface Smoke Screening System.

Step 1B

Choose the DI under which you plan to burn. Lower DIs (< 41) are not recommended because of poor smoke dispersion and DIs above 70 are not recommended because of the likelihood of fire control problems. Note that in Florida, the DI threshold for red-flag conditions is 75. Consider the DI chosen to be a tentative selection at this point. Go to Table 4 and use the tentatively selected DI to determine the maximum distance to which smoke is likely to be a problem based on the fuel category and firing technique chosen. Visible smoke may be present for this distance, although smoke can be smelled at much greater distances. Go to step 1C.

Table 4—Greatest distance of probable smoke impact from burns smaller than 50 acres

	Fuel category	Firing technique	Dispersion Index		
			41–50	51–60	61–70
			Impact distance in miles		
A	Grass, light understory (< 2-year rough) with no humus layer	Any firing technique	0.75	0.5	0.25
B	Nonwoody marsh fuels—rush, cattail, or sawgrass	Any firing technique	1.5	1.25	1
C	Palmetto/gallberry or waxmyrtle understory regardless of height	Backing fire	1.25	1	0.75
D[a][b]	Palmetto/gallberry or waxmyrtle understory regardless of height	Head, flank, or spot fires	4	3	2
E	Any other native understory fuel type regardless of height	Backing fire	1	0.75	0.5
F	Any other native understory fuel type under 3 feet high	Head, flank, or spot fires	1.5	1	0.75
G	Any other native understory fuel type over 3 feet high	Head, flank, or spot fires	2	1.5	1
H[a][b]	Melaleuca	Backing, flank, or spot fires	3	2	1
I	Exotic fuelbeds such as Casuarina without much understory	Any firing technique	2.5	2	1.5
J[a]	Scattered logging debris	Any firing technique	2.5	1.5	1
K[a]	Small dry piles	Any firing technique	3	2	1.5
L[c]	Large, wet, piled debris or windrows	Using any firing technique	Do not burn		

[a] Firing should be completed at least 2 hours before sunset because dispersion will rapidly deteriorate at dusk.
[b] Line headfires in 4- to 5-foot high palmetto, gallberry, waxmyrtle, or Melaleuca are very likely to result in severe overstory crown scorch.
[c] Windrows are the most polluting of all southern fuel types. They contain large fuels and dirt, and are compact which makes them very slow to dry and severely limits the amount of oxygen available for the combustion process. Dirt in piles or windrows will drastically increase the amount of smoke produced, and debris piles containing substantial amounts of dirt can smolder for weeks. To pass this screening system, any large piles of debris or windrows will have to be reconfigured into small round piles and allowed to dry with stumps removed or fireproofed.

Step 1C

Draw a line representing the centerline of the planned path of the smoke plume (transport wind direction) from the burn. Draw this line for the length of the impact distance determined from table 4. To allow for horizontal dispersion of smoke as well as shifts in wind direction, draw two additional lines out the same distance from the burn unit at 30-degree angles from the centerline of the transport wind direction. Connect the ends of the lines with arcs as in figures 2 and 3. Note that the transport wind direction and surface wind direction may differ on the day of the burn, e.g., if a seabreeze is present. In this case, plan for the change in smoke plume direction. When burning on a seabreeze, keep in mind that once the smoke plume is over water, it will likely drop to the surface and be blown back inland; the firing technique and pattern used should, thus, assure that the plume has dissipated by the time it might be blown back across the shoreline so that people will not be adversely impacted. When rechecking winds on the day of the burn, if forecast or actual surface winds are light (< 5 mph), replot the impact area using 45-degree angles.

If the planned burn is represented as a spot on the map you are using, draw as in figure 2 with a protractor and straight edge. If the map scale allows the burn dimensions to be drawn on the

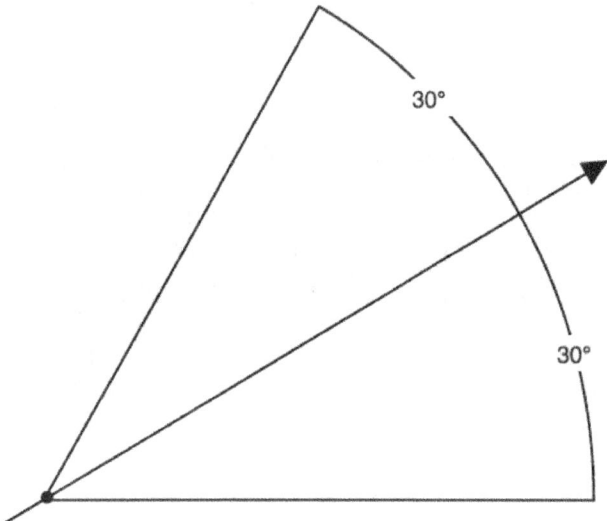

Figure 2— Plot of the probable smoke impact area when a point represents the burn.

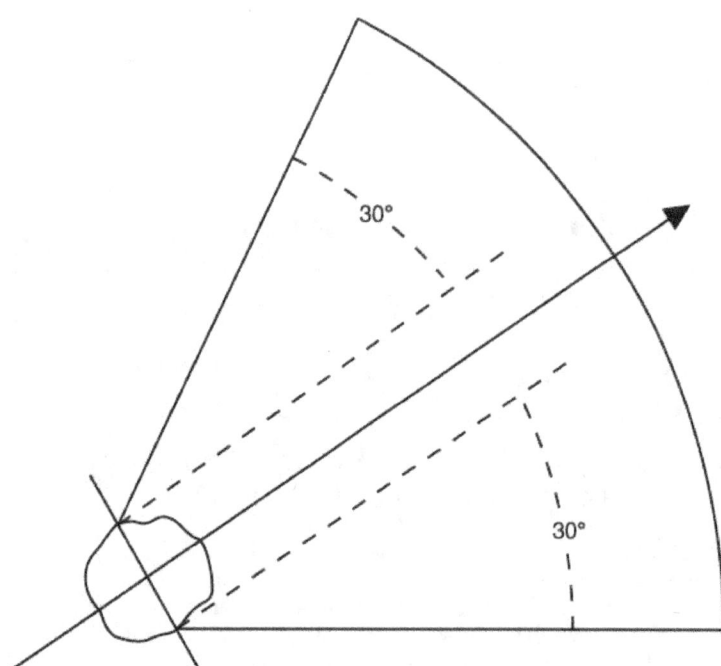

Figure 3— Plot of the probable smoke impact area when a figure other than a point represents the burn.

12

map, do so and draw as in figure 3. The result is the probable daytime smoke impact area. The heaviest smoke concentration will be along the centerline.

Figure 4 shows the application of step 1C to an example area. If the fuels present are grass, nonwoody marsh fuels, or less than a 2-year rough (fuel categories A and B), go to step 2, otherwise go to step 1D.

Step 1D

Next, go down-drainage the same distance determined from table 4 in step 1B. Draw a narrow area covering only the "bottom" or width of the

drainage area. This area may or may not lie wholly within the daytime smoke impact area. The result is your probable nighttime impact area due to the residual (smoldering) smoke produced. Note that the probable down-drainage nighttime smoke impact area shown in figure 4 can extend further than the distance suggested in table 4 because the smoke will be concentrated within this relatively narrow area and will seek the lowest elevation. If the smoke encounters heavy vegetation in the drainage, it will build up at that point. If an open area such as a pasture or field is also adjacent to the drainage at that point, the smoke will tend to spill over into this area if the terrain is fairly level.

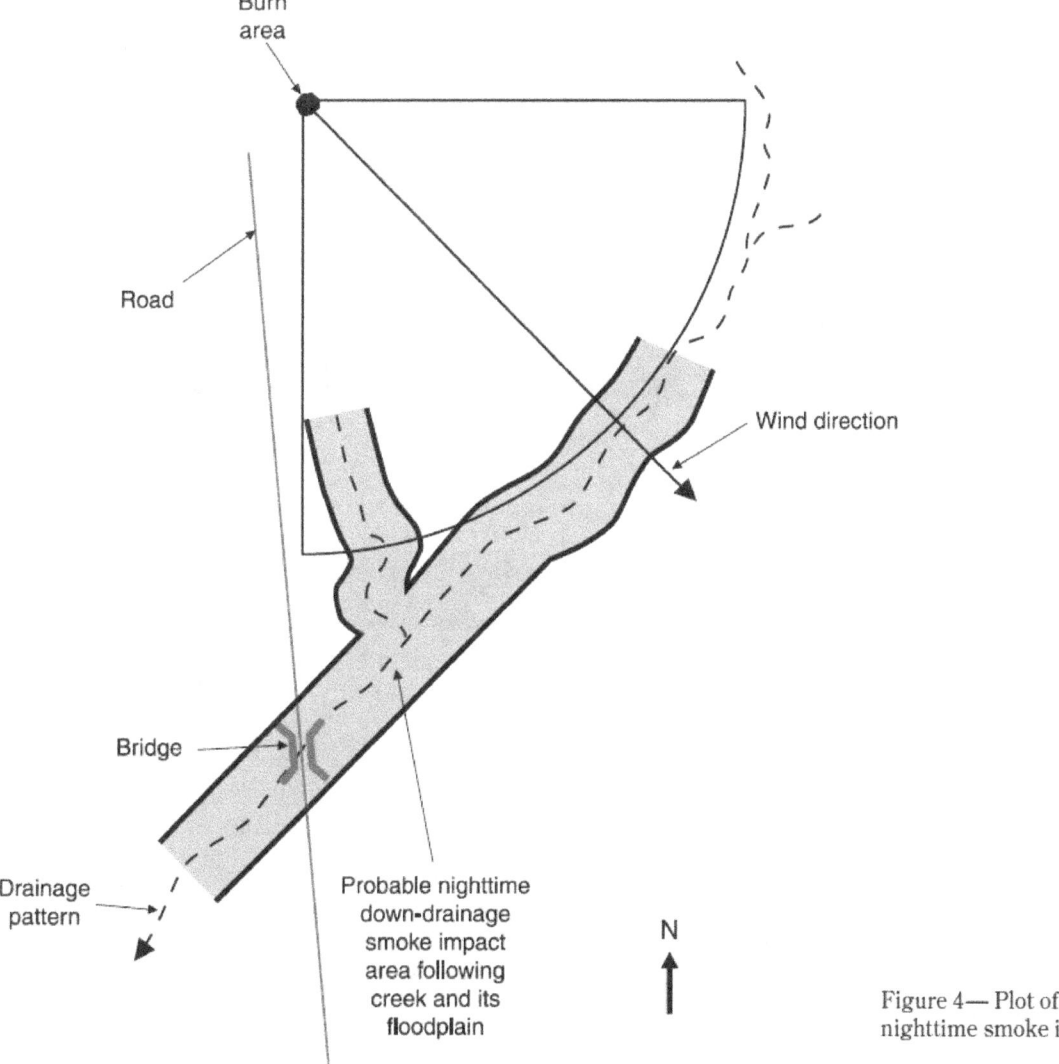

Figure 4— Plot of probable nighttime smoke impact area.

If your preburn site inspection suggests this could happen, monitor that area for smoke buildup after the burn, especially if an SSA is near the other end of the open area. Complete step 1D even if you plan to have the burn completely mopped up (out) at least 2 hours before dusk. Then, if for some reason residual smoke is present at dusk, you will know where it is likely to concentrate. Go to step 2.

Step 2—Identify Smoke Sensitive Areas

Step 2A

If the area to be burned contains organic soils that are likely to ignite, go to step 5B, otherwise go to step 2B.

Step 2B

Identify and mark any SSAs within 500 feet of the perimeter of the planned burn, regardless of direction from the fire as determined in step 1A above. Add these to the contact list in your written prescription. Make sure these SSAs are also discussed in the public relations section of your prescription. Go to step 2C.

Step 2C

Identify and list any SSAs located within the probable downwind impact area determined in step 1C. Go to step 2D.

Step 2D

Identify and list any SSAs located within the down-drainage impact area determined in step 1D. Go to step 2E.

Step 2E

If any SSAs were identified in 2B through 2D, mitigation is necessary as suggested in steps 3 and 4. Go to step 3.

If no SSAs are found, as described in steps 2A through 2D, then it is not likely you will have a smoke management problem. Go to step 5A.

Step 3—Dealing with Smoke Sensitive Areas within the 500-foot Buffer and/or First One-Fourth of the Impact Distance

Step 3A

Consider felling snags. If their retention is spelled out in the land management plan, follow standard procedures to keep them from igniting. Go to step 3B.

Step 3B

If the predicted or actual LVORI is 7, 8, 9, or 10, go to step 5B.

Step 3C

For fuel categories A through I: If any homes are within the 500-foot buffer, each homeowner must be personally contacted and informed that his or her home will likely be impacted by smoke. The landowner responses, e.g., that there are severe respiratory problems or fears that homes will be lost, should guide what actions are taken (include in the public relations plan).

Use the same fuel category selected in step 1B (table 4). Fuel category selections follow:

- Fuel category A or B: Go to step 3D
- Fuel category C, D, E, F, G, H, or I: Go to step 3E
- Fuel category J or K: Go to step 3F

Step 3D—Fuel Categories A and B

If no SSAs are within the 500-foot buffer zone or first one-fourth of the downwind smoke impact distance, go to step 4.

If any SSAs are within the buffer zone or first one-fourth of the predicted downwind smoke impact distance, a smoke problem resulting from the burn is a distinct possibility. First, try changing the prescribed wind direction or increasing the prescribed DI to minimize the number of SSAs that are within the smoke impact area.

If changing the wind direction or increasing the DI removes all SSAs from the buffer and first one-fourth of the downwind smoke impact distance, go to step 4. Otherwise, it is unavoidable that an SSA will be within the buffer zone or first one-fourth of the impact distance and mitigation will be necessary. Either mop up the burn completely (all smokes out) at least 1 hour before sunset or complete active burning at least 3 hours before sunset under one or more of the conditions listed below and mop up until dark:

- DI above 50
- MH above 2,500 feet
- Surface winds < 8 mph and transport wind speeds > 15 mph
- If the SSA is a road, mitigate by controlling or rerouting traffic during the burn

Continue by going to step 4.

Step 3E—Fuel Category C, D, E, F, G, H, or I

If an SSA is within 500 feet of the fire perimeter, regardless of the direction from the fire, divide the unit into two or more subunits, the smaller of which faces the SSA. An exception to creation of subunits can occur where smoke corridors are already established by county ordinance.

- The smaller subunit should have a depth such that the distance from the closest SSA to the back of the subunit is at least 500 feet on the edge of the burn facing the SSA. This edge should be delineated with a hard (plowed or raked) line or drainage ditch containing standing water. The burn manager may select a shorter distance in some specific situations, but much caution should be used. If the SSA is a road, closing the road during the burn removes this distance restriction. If the SSAs are homes, all homeowners must agree to the reduced distance with the full understanding that their residences could be impacted by drift smoke. In some uncommon situations, a Federal or State statute such as the Hawkins Law in Florida may allow you to ignore these guidelines, but we urge you to first carefully consider the potential public relations ramifications of such a decision.

- Burn this smaller subunit first toward the middle of the day, preferably when steady eye-level winds are blowing away from the SSA at speeds > 2 mph. If you desire to burn this subunit when eye-level winds are blowing toward the SSAs, consider specifying weather conditions and a firing technique that will facilitate lofting the smoke plume over the SSAs.

- If an SSA is down-drainage, make sure the subunit can be burned and completely mopped up (out) by dusk. This may require breaking the subunit into smaller (about 5-acre) blocks.

- If the SSA is a road, mitigate either by rerouting traffic during the burn or by stationing flaggers strategically. Be ready to extinguish the fire if necessary.

Once the smaller subunit is burned out, if no other SSAs are within 500 feet of the burn, address any SSAs within the first one-fourth of the impact area.

When multiple SSAs are within 500 feet of the burn unit on more than one side, your options are further constrained. If roads are present, control traffic flow; if homes are present, contact all residents and make sure they understand that their residences may be impacted by residual smoke. As a general rule, a residence should not be directly impacted by the plume, or impacted by residual smoke throughout the night. If you are not sure that *all* smoke will be pulled away from the SSAs as the remaining subunits are burned, divide the remaining subunits further.

If no SSAs are within the first one-fourth of the downwind smoke impact distance, go to step 4.

If any SSAs are within the first one-fourth of the downwind smoke impact distance, a smoke problem resulting from the burn is a distinct possibility. Change prescribed wind direction or increase DI to minimize the number of SSAs that lie within the first one-fourth of the downwind smoke impact distance.

If changing the prescribed wind direction or increasing the DI removes all SSAs from the first one-fourth of the downwind smoke impact distance impact area, go to step 4. If one or more SSAs remain within the first one-fourth of the impact distance, you must mitigate the problem. Burn and mop up completely (all smokes out) at least 1 hour before sunset, or complete active burning at least 3 hours (2 hours if using a backfire as described in the fourth bullet below) before sunset under one or more of the conditions listed below and mop up until dusk.

* DI above 50
* Divide unit into roughly 5-acre blocks and burn them separately
* Surface winds < 8 mph and transport wind speeds above 15 mph
* Use a backing fire and complete burn at least 2 hours before sunset. Begin mopup as soon as practicable after the flame front has passed.
* MH above 2,500 feet
* Keep stumps from igniting
* If the SSA is a road, mitigate by controlling or rerouting traffic during the burn

Continue by going to step 4.

Step 3F—Fuel Categories J and K

If any SSAs are within the 500-foot buffer zone, go to step 5B.

If no SSAs are within the first one-fourth of the downwind smoke impact distance, go to step 4.

If any SSAs are within the first one-fourth of the downwind smoke impact distance, a smoke problem resulting from the burn is a distinct possibility. Change prescribed wind direction or increase DI to minimize the number of SSAs that lie within the first one-fourth of the downwind smoke impact distance.

If changing the prescribed wind direction or increasing the DI removes all SSAs from the first one-fourth of the downwind smoke impact distance, go to step 4. If an SSA is unavoidable within the first one-fourth of the impact distance, you must mitigate the problem. Burn and mop up completely (all smokes out) at least 1 hour before sunset. The following conditions will facilitate smoke dispersal:

* DI above 50
* Keep stumps from igniting
* Divide the unit into roughly 5-acre blocks and burn these subunits separately
* Burn when the MH is above 2,500 feet
* Surface winds < 8 mph and transport wind speeds > 15 mph
* If the SSA is a road, control or reroute traffic during the burn

Continue by going to step 4.

Step 4—Dealing with Smoke Sensitive Areas within the Last Three-Fourths of the Impact Distance

Step 4A

Select the same fuel category used in step 3. Selections are grouped by fuel category as follows:

* Fuel category A or B: Go to step 5A

- Fuel category C, D, E, F, G, H, or I: Go to step 4B
- Fuel category J or K: Go to step 4C

Step 4B—Fuel Category C, D, E, F, G, H, or I

Either:

- Complete firing at least 3 hours before sunset and mop up a minimum of 500 feet in from the downwind edge of the burned area, or
- Use a backing fire and completely mop up the burn at least 1 hour before sunset. Begin mopup soon after the flame front has passed and continue until dusk

If residual smoke is present at dusk, monitor all night and be prepared to act if a roadway is impacted.

Continue by going to step 5A.

Step 4C—Fuel Category J or K

If no interstate or major highways are within 2 miles down-drainage, consider the list of potential measures below. Implement as many as practical to mitigate potential smoke problems.

- Burn when the DI is above 50
- Reduce the size of the area to be burned
- Complete firing at least 3 hours before sunset
- Mop up as needed
- Burn when surface winds are < 8 mph and transport wind speeds are > 15 mph
- Monitor smoke all night and be prepared to act if a roadway is impacted
- Keep stumps from igniting
- Burn when MH is above 2,500 feet

If interstate or other major highways are within 2 miles down-drainage, divide the unit into subunits and implement as many of the above measures as practical.

Continue by going to step 5A.

Step 5—Interpreting Screening System Results

Step 5A—All Requirements Met

If all the requirements in the smoke screening system have been met to this point, it is not likely that the prescribed fire will result in a smoke problem if the maximum burn unit size is < 50 acres. Keep in mind that as the DI class under which the burn is conducted increases, fire intensity and suppression become more challenging. In order to use this WUI screening system for burn units > 50 acres, you must subdivide the unit into blocks of 50 acres or less to conform with the underlying assumptions used in developing this system.

If you proceed and a smoke problem is encountered, please notify others of the problem you encountered, e.g., your prescribed fire council, and get word back to Scott Goodrick with the Southern Research Station, Disturbance Work Unit, Smoke Management Team located in Athens, GA, at the following Web address: http://www.srs.fs.fed.us/smoke/contacts.htm so that the situation can be examined and changes to the screening system can be made as appropriate.

Step 5B—Not All Requirements Met

If not all smoke screening system requirements have been met, consider the following options:

- Do not burn. Use a mechanical, chemical, or biotic alternative instead
- Change the prescription to meet the requirements
- Reduce the burn unit size to roughly 2-acre blocks, burn with low surface winds, and mop up completely by dark

There may be rare situations where a proposed burn will not pass any smoke screening system under the best dispersion conditions, but the use of fire is still the preferred alternative (e.g., see

Miller and Wade 2003). In such cases, the burn manager should take all the extra steps listed below and then proceed with extreme caution:

- All homeowners within the potential impact area agree to tolerate any temporary inconveniences associated with the intended burn [unless burning within a legalized smoke corridor or under a state statute such as the Hawkins Law (Florida Statute 590.125)]

- Local law enforcement and government officials are kept informed and agree with the necessity of the burn

- All homeowners are contacted within several weeks of the burn and informed of the planned burn date, anticipated ignition time, burn duration, and mopup time. Homeowners should be given the address of a Web site where any schedule changes will be posted

- In the above situations, it is still recommended that:

  - Photos be taken before, during and after the fire including any residual smoke indicating time of photo.

  - The burn be completely mopped up and declared out before burn personnel leave

  - If residual smoke is present at dusk, monitor it throughout the night

If some conditions are marginal, smoke could still be a problem; consider reducing the size of the burn. On the other hand, it may be possible to burn without causing a smoke intrusion even though this screening system indicates otherwise. Situations where this is likely the case include:

- The distance to the SSA is close to the maximum impact distance

- The amount of available fuel is less than average

- The fuel is very dry and the fuel bed is loosely arranged

- The only downwind SSA is close to the end of the arc constructed in step 1C. Note that the heaviest smoke concentration will be along the centerline

The decision to proceed with the burn or to delay it until another time is up to the manager of the prescribed burn. Remember that ideal conditions at ignition time can change during the burn. This will most likely happen to every prescribed fire manager as a result of conditions that are not anticipated or not as forecasted. When such a situation occurs, follow three guiding principles:

1. Use common sense—Do what a prudent individual would do

2. Use integrity—Do the right thing

3. Keep good records—Have and follow a written plan and document all changes to it as they are made

Hot Tip

This smoke screening system does not take into account other sources of smoke that may already be reducing visibility in the area.

Minimum background visibility around the intended burn site should be at least 5 miles.

Acknowledgments

This screening system is based on the screening system developed by the Southern Forest Fire Laboratory Staff (1976) and revisions to it as dictated by extensive field use over the next several decades which can be accessed at www.pfmt.org/fire, a Web site maintained by Auburn University. The lead author modified this revised product at the request of the Florida Division of Forestry to develop a smoke management unit to be taught at an advanced training course for certified prescribed burners. Development of this course entitled "Implementing Prescribed Fire in the Wildland Urban Interface" was facilitated by Don Carlton with the Washington Institute. The first draft of this unit was critically reviewed by the course faculty and suggested modifications hammered out in discussion with faculty members, notably Jim Brenner, Barry Coulliette, Rich Gordon, John Kern, and Judy Turner with the Florida Division of Forestry; Steven Miller with the St. Johns Water Management District; Caroline Noble with the National Park Service; and Walt Thomson with The Nature Conservancy. Don Carlton produced original electronic versions of figures 1 and 4. This and all other evolving units were then presented in a dry run to a group of hand picked experienced burners and further modified in light of their comments. In February 2003, the smoke unit was distributed to the faculty and participants of the dry run as well as to remaining Florida Division of Forestry Forest Area Supervisors and Prescribed Burn Team Leaders; these people were asked to use and evaluate the screening system. Based on the positive feedback from those who used and evaluated this screening system over the next 2 years and the lack of any reported problems, it was decided to formalize and publish this WUI screening system for use throughout the South. The authors also wish to thank Jim Brenner with the Florida Division of Forestry, Scott Goodrick with the USDA Forest Service, and Paul Watts with the South Carolina Forestry Commission who reviewed this manuscript and made valuable contributions. Rick Henion with the Maine Forest Service produced clip art used in this report.

Literature Cited

Hardy, C.C.; Ottmar, R.D.; Peterson, J.L. [and others], comps., eds. 2001. Smoke management guide for prescribed burning and wildland fire: 2001 edition. PMS 420–2. Boise, ID: National Wildfire Coordinating Group. 226 p.

Lavdas, L.G. 1986. An atmospheric dispersion index for prescribed burning. Research Pap. SE–256. Asheville, NC: U.S. Department of Agriculture Forest Service, Southeastern Forest Experiment Station. 33 p.

Lavdas, L.G. 1996. Improving control of smoke from prescribed fire using low visibility occurrence risk index. Southern Journal of Applied Forestry. 20(1): 10-14.

Miller, S.R.; Wade, D. 2003. Re-introducing fire at the urban/wild-land interface: planning for success. Forestry. 76 (2): 253-260.

Sandberg, D.V.; Ottmar, R.D.; Peterson, J.L.; Core, J. 2002. Wildland fire in ecosystems: effects of fire on air. Gen. Tech. Rep. RMRS–GTR–42. Ogden, UT: U.S. Department of Agriculture Forest Service, Rocky Mountain Research Station. 79 p. Vol. 5.

Southern Forest Fire Laboratory Staff. 1976. Southern forestry smoke management guidebook. Gen. Tech. Rep. SE–10. Asheville, NC: U.S. Department of Agriculture Forest Service, Southeastern Forest Experiment Station. 140 p. Available on the Web at: http://www.srs.fs.usda.gov/pubs/viewpub. jsp?index=683. [Date accessed: March 2007].

Appendix A

Some Federal and Florida Air Quality Laws and Rules

Federal Clean Air Act

- The Clean Air Act (as amended in 1987 and 1997) is a legal system designed to protect human health and welfare.

- Several sections of the Clean Air Act have smoke management implications.

- The Clean Air Act establishes minimum requirements, which must be met nationwide, but States may establish additional requirements.

- The various acts, amendments, and regulations can be found on the U.S. Environmental Protection Agency (EPA) Web site at http://www.epa.gov/epahome/laws.htm.

National Ambient Air Quality Standards

- EPA has established National Ambient Air Quality Standards (NAAQS) for the following air pollutants that are produced in wildland fires:

  – Particulate matter

  – Nitrogen dioxide

  – Ozone

  – Carbon monoxide

- Air quality monitors are located throughout Florida and maintained by the Florida Department of Environmental Protection, Division of Air Quality

- These monitors are often located at the wildland-urban interface, so they are much more likely to be impacted by smoke at levels exceeding the NAAQS

Florida Statutes and Rules Pertaining to Smoke Management

- Burn authorization is required from Florida Division of Forestry.

- Florida Division of Forestry may restrict or cancel authorizations if burning under rule 5I–2 of the Florida Administrative Code creates a condition that is deleterious to health, safety, or general welfare.

continued

Appendix A (continued)

Florida Statutes and Rules Pertaining to Smoke Management (continued)

- Florida Division of Forestry authorizations require burning to be done between 9 a.m. and 1 hour before sunset or at other times when conditions warrant. For certified burners, this time period is extended to 1 hour after sunset.

- Smoke from a burn must not reduce visibility on public roadways to < 500 feet.

- A burn must not violate local laws, rules, regulations, or ordinances.

- An updated synopsis of current Florida statutes and rules governing fire management can be found on the Florida Division of Forestry wildland fire Web site at http://www.fl-dof.com/wildfire/index.

Appendix B

How to Reduce the Smoke Impact from Prescribed Burns

Prescribed burning can be used to achieve many resource objectives, but it pollutes the air. Burn managers have an obligation to minimize this pollution. If this obligation is ignored, prescribed burners can be held liable for smoke-related damage if smoke causes accidents or other problems. To reduce the impact of smoke at the wildland-urban interface (WUI), heed the following advice:

1. Smoke management should be based on common sense and integrity.

2. Prepare a written burn plan well in advance of the burn.

3. Define objectives. Be sure you have clear resource objectives and have considered both onsite and offsite environmental impacts.

4. Develop a smoke management plan and attach it (along with any calculations) to the written burn prescription.

5. Fire weather and smoke management forecasts are available through State forestry agencies. Be sure to use them. Such information is necessary to predict smoke production and movement as well as fire behavior. If the forestry weather outlook does not agree reasonably well with the radio or television forecast, find out why before proceeding.

6. In States that have a forestry agency fire meteorologist, such as Florida and Georgia, consider asking for a spot weather forecast. Contact information can be obtained by calling your local forestry unit.

7. Don't burn during pollution alerts or stagnant conditions. Smoke tends to stay near the ground at such times, will not disperse readily, and will exacerbate existing conditions. Many fire weather meteorologists include pollution alerts and stagnation information in their daily forecasts. The mixing height should be at least 1,700 feet and transport windspeed should be at least 9 miles per hour (mph) when prescribed burns are conducted.

8. Comply with air pollution control regulations. Know the regulations that apply at the proposed burn site when you write the prescription. Check with your State fire control agency if in doubt.

9. Burn when conditions are good for rapid dispersion. Ideally, the atmosphere should be slightly unstable so smoke will rise and dissipate, but not so unstable as to cause a control problem. Again, your local forestry agency can help. Some States use category day based on the ventilation rate to describe smoke transport and dispersion conditions, but the Dispersion Index (DI) is a better indicator.

10. Reassess a decision to burn at the WUI when the daytime DI is forecast to be below 41 and use increasing caution as it approaches 70.

11. Use caution when within 500 feet of smoke-sensitive areas (SSAs) or upwind of them. Burning should be done when wind will carry smoke away from public roads, airports, hospitals, schools, and

continued

How to Reduce the Smoke Impact from Prescribed Burns (continued)

populated areas. This is often not possible at the WUI so extreme care must be exercised to minimize the impact on SSAs. Do not burn if a hospital, school (in session), or airport (unless departures and arrivals can be temporarily suspended) is within one-half mile downwind of the proposed burn.

12. Work with local law enforcement personnel to manage or reroute traffic on downwind roads. Avoid heavy traffic periods such as noontime and late afternoon. Monitor for residual smoke on roads within 1 mile of the burn in all directions until the fire is declared out.

13. Develop and implement a public relations plan that includes personal contact with all homeowners and businesses within one-half mile of the burn unit. Check for any health issues, especially respiratory problems, and schedule the burn when any residents with relevent health problems will be gone overnight; work with such residents to find a place to stay or consider paying to put them in a motel at least the first night postburn. Use firing techniques and ignition patterns that minimize offsite fly ash, make sure windows in all houses likely to be impacted are closed on the day of the burn. Make sure inside pets are removed during the burn. Make sure all potentially affected residents understand that prescribed fire reduces the hazardous accumulation of fuels as well as air pollution from wildfires.

14. When burn units have adjacent SSAs on three or more sides or when they are down-drainage, try to keep burn units smaller than 5 acres so they can be burned and completely mopped up within a single day. It is much better to divide a 20-acre block into four 5-acre blocks and burn and mop up each on a separate day than to burn all 20 acres as a single unit and impact adjacent homes over the next several days until mopup is complete.

15. If the unit has homes on all sides (no smoke corridor), do not burn when DI is < 41. The larger the area being burned, the greater the amount of particulate matter put into the air, and the longer visibility is reduced downwind. However, if weather conditions are good for rapid smoke dispersion, as when the DI is above 50, it is often better from a smoke management standpoint to burn the whole area at one time using a firing technique that creates a convection column to loft the smoke over nearby structures and roads. Remember that creation of a convection column during the flaming phase does little to mitigate production, dilution, or dispersion of residual smoke.

16. Fine fuels carry a fire. Removal of large (100- and 1000-hr) dead, down fuels will have little effect on reducing the fire hazard at the WUI. Once they are ignited, however, large fuels generate smoke for extended periods. Choose burning conditions that will minimize ignition of

How to Reduce the Smoke Impact from Prescribed Burns (continued)

large fuels. Ideally, burn when they are wet and fine fuels are dry. Headfires are less likely to ignite larger fuels because they have a shorter residence time. If large fuels present are sound, consider the practicability of physically removing them prior to the burn.

17. Check moisture content of fine fuels and lower litter by feeling with your hands. Upper litter should be fairly dry and lower litter too wet to burn.

18. Use the Keetch-Byram Drought Index (also called the Cumulative Severity Index). If large-diameter fuels are present, reconsider a decision to burn when it is above 400 or use a moisture meter to make sure the moisture content of large dead fuels is above 20 percent.

19. If snags or stumps are present, take measures to keep them from igniting.

20. Use a test fire to confirm smoke behavior. Set it in or adjacent to (if fuel conditions are comparable) the area proposed for burning, away from roads or other edge effects, and make sure it is large enough for you to assess smoke behavior.

21. Consider using a backfire at least near homes. Although slower and more expensive, a backing fire produces less smoke (only about one-third of the particulate emissions generated by a heading fire). Substantially less smoldering combustion takes place in backing fires, and smoldering combustion

emits about five times as much particulate matter as flaming combustion emits.

22. Burn during the middle of the day when possible. Atmospheric conditions are generally most favorable for smoke dispersion at this time.

23. Do *not* ignite organic soils. If they are present at the WUI, use another method to reduce hazardous fuel accumulations. The only exception is if the organic soil is confined to depressional ponds, in which case burn only when they are full (no organic soil above water). It is virtually impossible to put out an organic soil fire without submerging it in water. It will smoke for weeks despite control efforts, creating severe smoke problems for miles around. Such fires can also re-ignite unconsumed surface fuels days or weeks later, resulting in a wildfire.

24. As a rule of thumb, do not burn at the WUI after sunset because smoke drift is almost impossible to predict when surface winds die down. One exception is the night after a frontal passage when surface winds will be above 4 mph and relative humidity will stay below 70 percent.

25. *Never* burn at the WUI under an inversion, no matter how small the unit.

26. A nighttime smoke patrol is recommended when a burn at the WUI is still smoking at sundown.

27. Anticipate down-drainage smoke flow. Atmospheric conditions tend to become

continued

Appendix B (continued)

How to Reduce the Smoke Impact from Prescribed Burns (continued)

stable at night. Stable conditions tend to keep smoke near the ground. In addition, downslope winds generally prevail at night even on gradual slopes unless surface winds are stronger. Thus, smoke will flow down-drainage and concentrate in low areas. When relative humidity rises above 80 percent and smoke is present, the formation of fog becomes increasingly likely as moisture condenses on the smoke particles. There are few satisfactory solutions to these problems, so try to avoid burning at the WUI late in the day.

28. Start mopup soon after the flame front passes to reduce the impact on visibility. Use water, ideally with foam, to extinguish duff around tree stems, and all stumps, snags, and logs.

29. Have an emergency plan. Be prepared to extinguish a prescribed burn if it is not burning according to plan, or if weather conditions change. Have warning signs on site. If wind direction changes, be prepared to quickly direct traffic on affected roads until traffic control personnel arrive.

Appendix C

Suggested Reading

Achtemeier, G.L. 2001. Simulating nocturnal smoke movement. Fire Management Today. 61: 28-33.

Battye, R.; Bauer, B.; MacDonald, G. 1999. Features of prescribed fire and smoke management rules for Western and Southern States. Chapel Hill, NC: EC/R Inc. Contract 68–D–98–026. Prepared for: U.S. Environmental Protection Agency

Breyfogle, S.; Ferguson, S.A. 1996. User assessment of smoke dispersion models for wildland biomass burning. Gen. Tech. Rep. PNW–GTR–379. Portland, OR: U.S. Department of Agriculture Forest Service, Pacific Northwest Research Station. 30 p.

Bryan, D.C., ed. 1997. Conference proceedings: environmental regulation & prescribed fire: legal and social challenges. Tallahassee, FL: Florida State University, Center for Professional Development. 246 p.

Eshee, W.D. 1997. Legal implications of using prescribed fire. In: Environmental regulation & prescribed fire: legal and social challenges. Tallahassee, FL: Florida State University, Center for Professional Development: 126-130.

Harms, M.F.; Lavdas, L.G. 1997. Draft user's guide to VSMOKE–GIS for workstations. Research Pap. SRS–6. Asheville, NC: U.S. Department of Agriculture Forest Service, Southern Research Station. 41 p.

Lavdas, L.G. 1996. Program VSMOKE – user manual. Gen. Tech. Rep. SRS–6. Asheville, NC: U.S. Department of Agriculture Forest Service, Southern Research Station. 147 p.

Lavdas, L.G; Hauck, C.A. 1991. Climatology of selected prescribed fire highway safety parameters for Florida. In: Proceedings, 11th conference on fire and forest meteorology. SAF Publ. 91–04. Bethesda, MD: Society of American Foresters: 564-571.

Laverty, L.; Williams, J. 2000. Protecting people and sustaining resources in fire-adapted ecosystems: a cohesive strategy. Washington, DC: U.S. Department of Agriculture Forest Service. 85 p.

Malm, W.C. 2000. Introduction to visibility. CA–2350–97. Ft. Collins, CO: Colorado State University, Cooperative Institute for Research in the Atmosphere: T097-04, T098-06.

Mobley, H.E. 1989. Summary of smoke-related accidents in the South from prescribed fire (1979–1988). Tech. Release 90–R–11. American Pulpwood Association.

U.S. Department of the Interior; U.S. Department of Agriculture. 1995. Federal wildland fire management policy and program review. Final Rep. Boise, ID: Bureau of Land Management. 45 p.

U.S. Department of the Interior; U.S. Department of Agriculture; U.S. Department of Energy [and others]. 2001. Review and update of the 1995 Federal wildland fire management policy. Boise, ID: Bureau of Land Management. 78 p.

continued

Suggested Reading (continued)

U.S. Environmental Protection Agency. 1998. Interim air quality policy on wildland and prescribed fires. [Place of publication unknown]: U.S. Environmental Protection Agency, Office of Air Quality Planning and Standards. 29 p.

U.S. Environmental Protection Agency. 2000. National ambient air quality standards (NAAQS). http://www.epa.gov/air/criteria. html. [Date accessed: March 2007].

U.S. Environmental Protection Agency. 2000. Wildland fire issues group. http://www. epa.gov/ttncaaa1/faca/fa08.html. [Date accessed: March 2007].

Wade, D.D.; Lunsford, J.D. 1989. A guide for prescribed fire in southern forests. Tech. Publ. R8–TP11. Atlanta: U.S. Department of Agriculture Forest Service, Southern Region. 56 p. [Reprinted by National Wildfire Coordinating Group. Available from National Interagency Fire Center, Boise, ID.]

www.ingramcontent.com/pod-product-compliance
Lightning Source LLC
Chambersburg PA
CBHW080733290526

45790CB00008B/3172